Fantastic Fliers

COMBAT AIRCRAFT

TOP THAT! Kids™

Published by Top That! Publishing plc
Tide Mill Way, Woodbridge, Suffolk, IP12 IAP, UK
www.topthatpublishing.com
Copyright © 2003 Top That! Publishing plc
Top That! is a Registered Trademark of Top That! Publishing plc

FOLDING TIPS

BEFORE YOU BEGIN ANY OF THE PROJECTS IN THIS BOOK, HERE ARE SOME HELPFUL TIPS THAT WILL MAKE YOUR FOLDING EASIER:

- *Before you start folding, make sure your paper is the correct shape.*

- *Fold on a flat surface, like a table or a book.*

- *Make your folds and cuts neat and accurate.*

- *Crease your folds into place by running your thumbnail along them.*

- *Carefully score along the marked lines using safety scissors and a ruler. This will make folding easier, especially as the lines become obscured towards the end of the model-making.*

SYMBOLS AND BASIC FOLDING PROCEDURES

These symbols show the direction in which paper should be folded. Although you'll not use them all in this book, you can use them to make up your own planes.

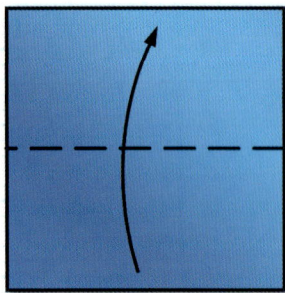

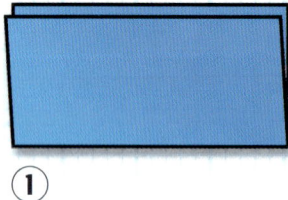

1. VALLEY FOLD (FOLD IN FRONT)

2. MOUNTAIN FOLD (FOLD BEHIND)

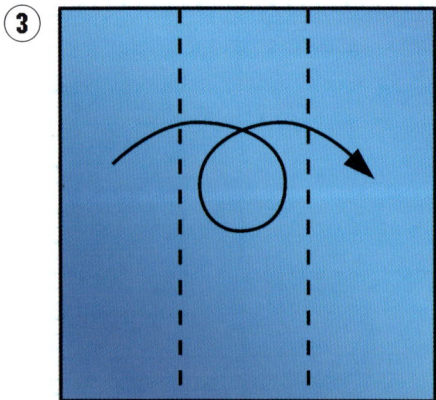

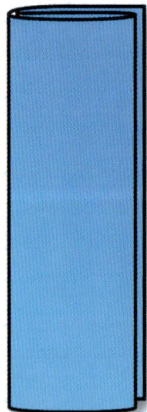

3. FOLD OVER AND OVER

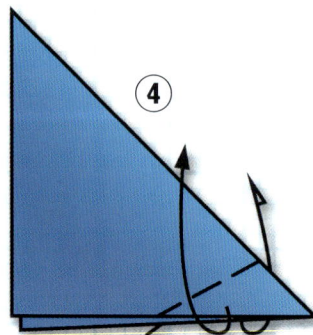

4. OUTSIDE REVERSE FOLD

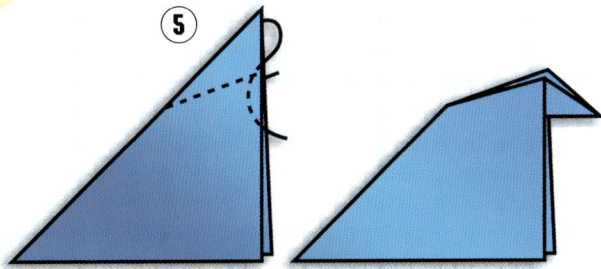

5. INSIDE REVERSE FOLD

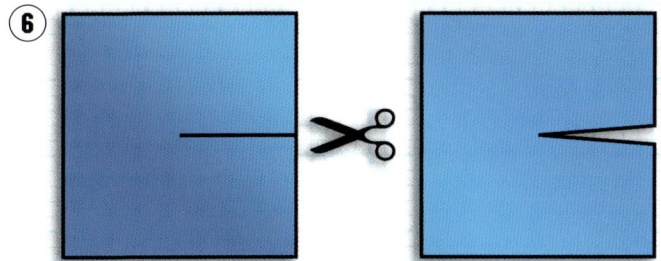

6. CUT

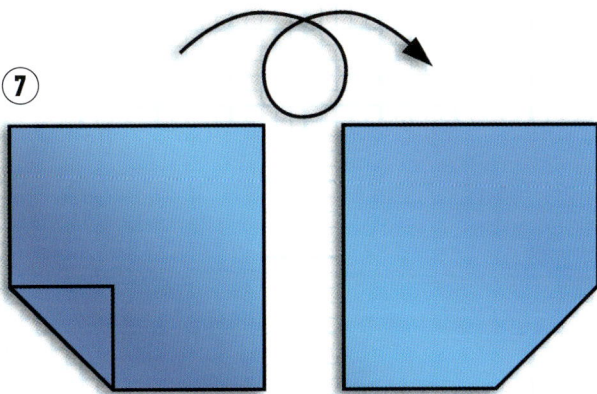

7. TURN PAPER OVER

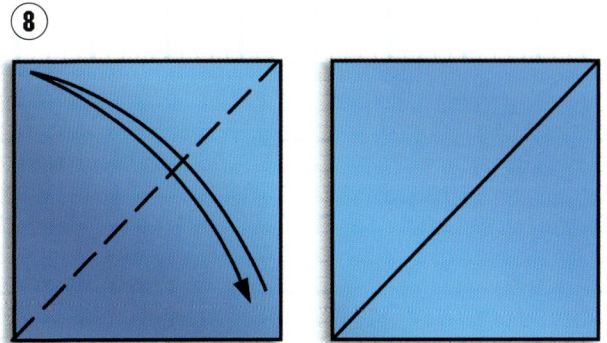

8. FOLD AND UNFOLD

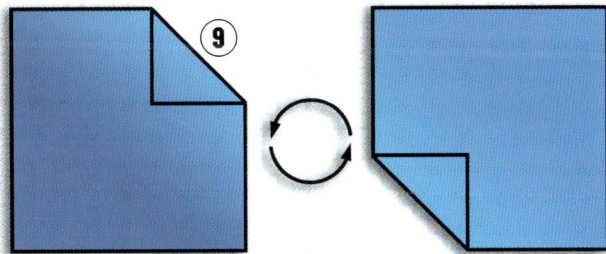

9. TURN PAPER ROUND

10. OPEN OUT

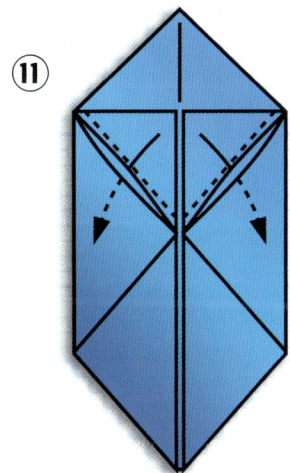

11. INSERT

FANTASTIC FLIERS FACT

A hypersonic jet engine flew at over seven times the speed of sound over the Australian desert, in 2002.

BAe HUNTER UK

THIS FEARLESS COMBAT FIGHTER IS A MUST ON ANY WAR MISSION.
USE THE PRINTED PAGE NUMBERED 1 AT THE BACK OF THIS BOOK.

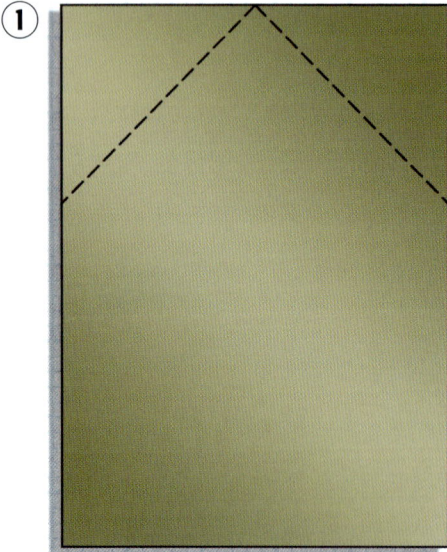

1. Fold in the two top corners along the dotted lines using valley folds.

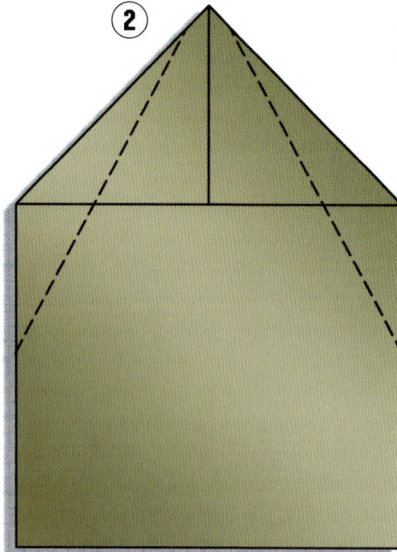

2. Fold along the two diagonal dotted lines, again using valley folds.

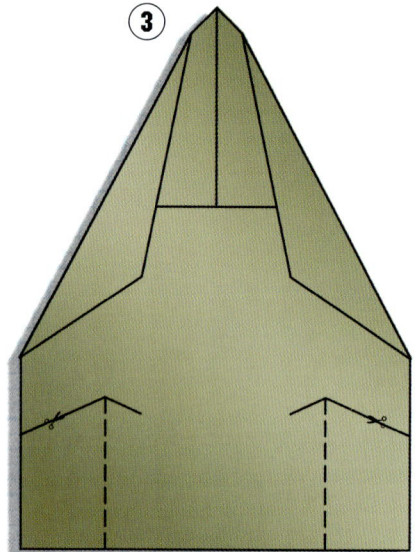

3. Cut along the two solid angled lines as shown. Now fold in the two flaps, using valley folds, along the dotted lines. Keep these flaps firmly in place throughout the remaining stages.

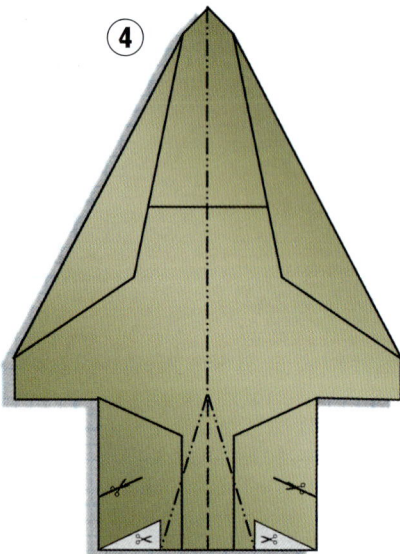

4. Make mountain folds along the three dashed lines running down the centre of the plane. Make sure you form a short valley fold between the two diagonal mountain folds at the rear of the plane. Cut away the two rear triangles to shape the tail fins. Cut the two small solid lines.

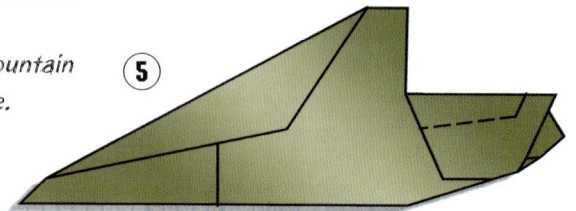

5. Form the shape of the wings and tail by making the remaining valley folds along both sides of the plane.

Hold the base of your plane between your thumb and forefinger and throw quite firmly.

FANTASTIC FLIERS FACT
Modern fighter jets can do amazing things. The MIG 29 can practically stop in mid-air — or shoot straight upwards.

BAe HAWK 200

ANOTHER AMAZING AIRCRAFT MADE IN A FEW EASY STEPS.
USE THE PRINTED PAGE NUMBERED 2 AT THE BACK OF THIS BOOK.

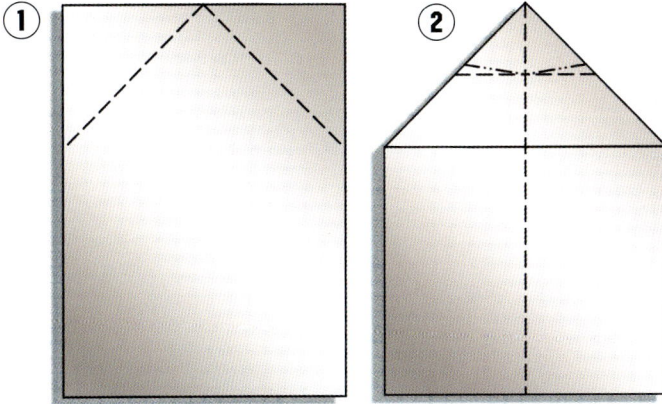

1. Fold in the two top corners along the dotted lines using valley folds.

2. Fold down the top triangle along the dotted line using a valley fold. Next, make two mountain folds along the diagonal dashed lines by folding the pointed tip back on itself. Firmly fold the plane down its centre, using a valley fold, ensuring that the folds in the pointed tip stay securely tucked in place.

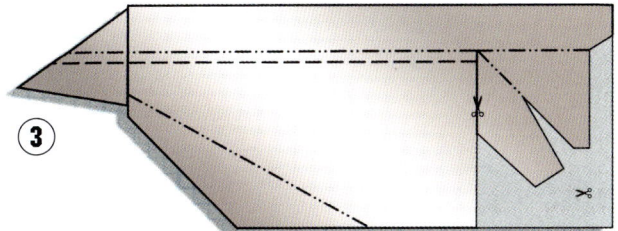

3. Form the tail shape by cutting along the solid lines, as shown. To create the plane's body and wings, bend mountain folds and valley folds along the dotted lines, as shown.

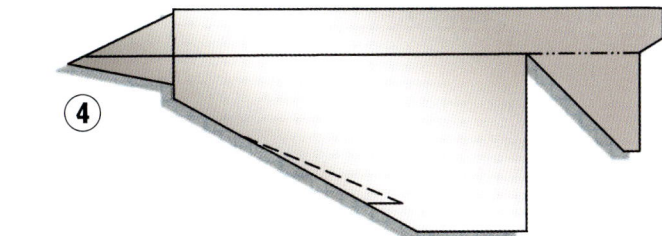

4. Make a cut along the bottom of the wings on the solid line, as shown. Valley fold along the diagonal lines on both sides, to form the wings. Tuck the tail up through the slit at the rear of the plane using a series of inward facing folds, as shown (right). Bend down the tail fins.

Hold the base of the plane between your thumb and forefinger about 5 cm from the front and gently throw it straight forward.

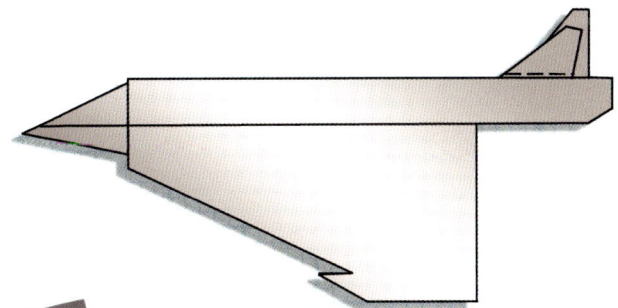

FANTASTIC FLIERS FACT
The Sopwith Camel was one of World War I's greatest fighter aircraft, with around 3,000 combat victories.

BAe HARRIER GR MK7

PREPARE FOR COMBAT WITH THIS GREAT FIGHTER PLANE.
USE THE PRINTED PAGE NUMBERED 3 AT THE BACK OF THIS BOOK.

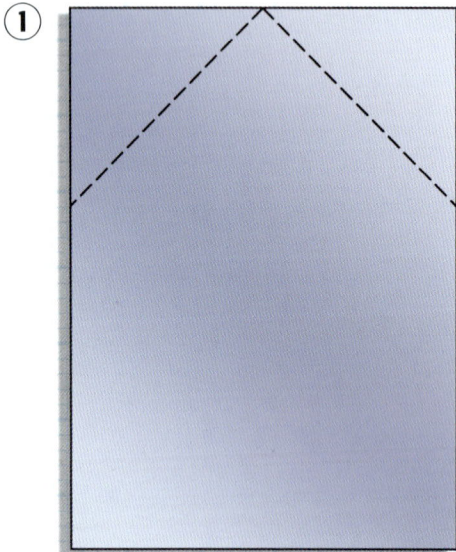

1. Fold in the two top corners along the dotted lines using valley folds.

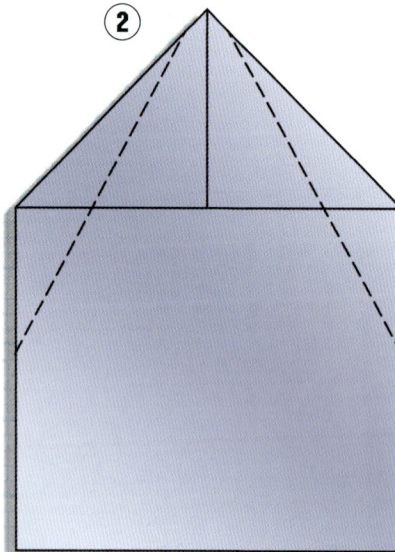

2. Fold along the two diagonal dotted lines, again using valley folds.

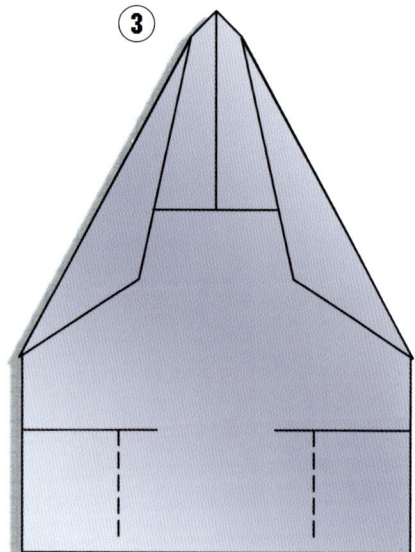

3. Cut along the two short horizontal lines on either side of the plane. Then fold in these tabs along the vertical lines.

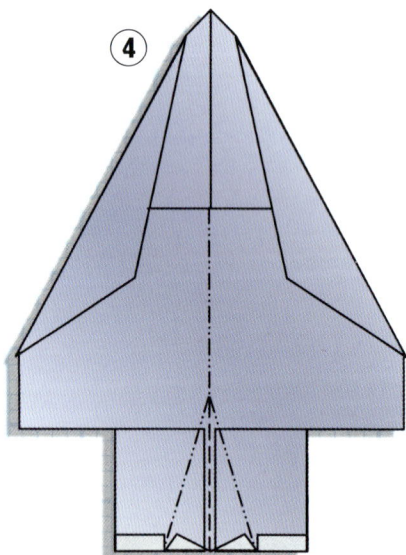

4. Cut along the bottom solid lines to cut a rectangle from the rear of the plane. Make mountain folds along the three dashed lines running down the centre of the plane. Make sure you form a short valley fold between the two diagonal mountain folds at the rear of the plane.

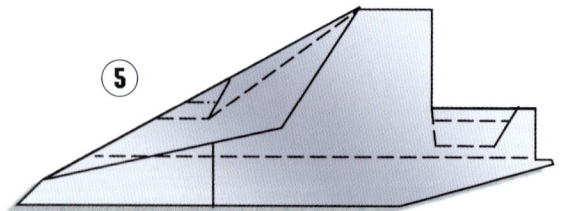

5. Make short cuts along the solid lines on the wing and tail areas. Using valley folds, form the shape of the plane by folding along the lines, as shown.

To fly your plane hold it between your forefinger and thumb about 10 cm from the front, and throw it gently.

FANTASTIC FLIERS FACT
The Spitfire had a hi-tech metal skinned body. Its propeller blades could be set at different angles to help it at take-off or in high speed flying.

EF-2000

THIS STREAMLINED FIGHTER WILL GLIDE INTO ACTION WITH THE GREATEST OF EASE. USE THE PRINTED PAGE NUMBERED 4 AT THE BACK OF THIS BOOK.

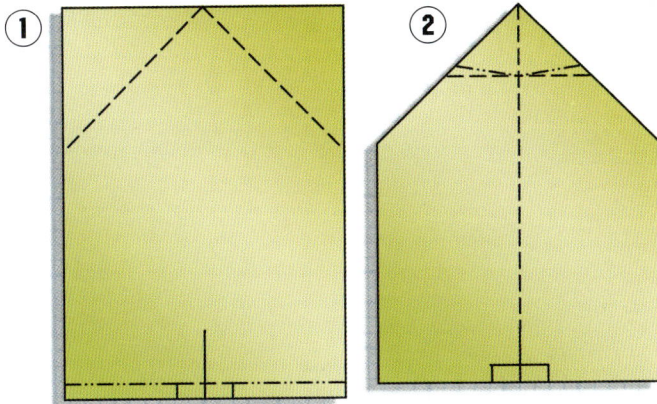

1. Fold in the two top corners along the dotted lines using valley folds. Make three vertical cuts at the bottom along the solid lines. Bend the outside flaps under using mountain folds. Then bend the inside flaps up by using valley folds.

2. Fold down the top triangle using a valley fold. Next, make two mountain folds along the diagonal lines by folding the pointed tip back on itself. Firmly fold the plane down its centre, using a valley fold, ensuring that the folds in the pointed tip stay securely tucked in place.

3. Using the solid lines as your guide, cut away the area around the tail of the plane. Make a series of mountain folds and valley folds to form the shape of the plane, as shown. Tuck the tail up through the slit at the rear of the plane using a mountain fold on each side, as shown.

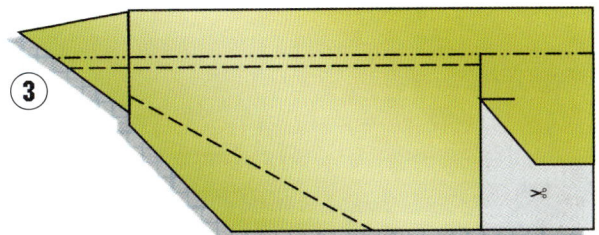

4. Fold up the wing tips using valley folds along the dotted lines. Secure the tail by tucking the flap from one side around the other and interlock them.

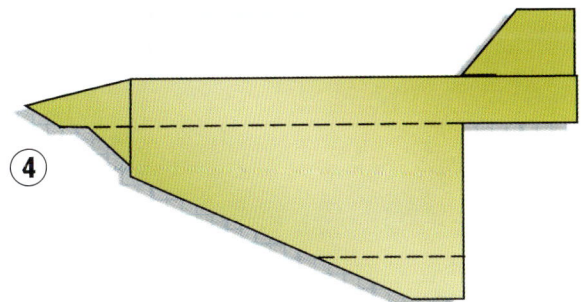

To fly the plane hold it 5 cm from the front and throw it gently forwards.

FANTASTIC FLIERS FACT
The P51 Mustang was a fast and furious fighter. It was also amazing because of its range. It could fly 1,500 miles.

LOCKHEED F-117A

THIS UNUSUAL LOOKING PLANE MAKES A GREAT FIGHTER.
USE THE PRINTED PAGE NUMBERED 5 AT THE BACK OF THIS BOOK.

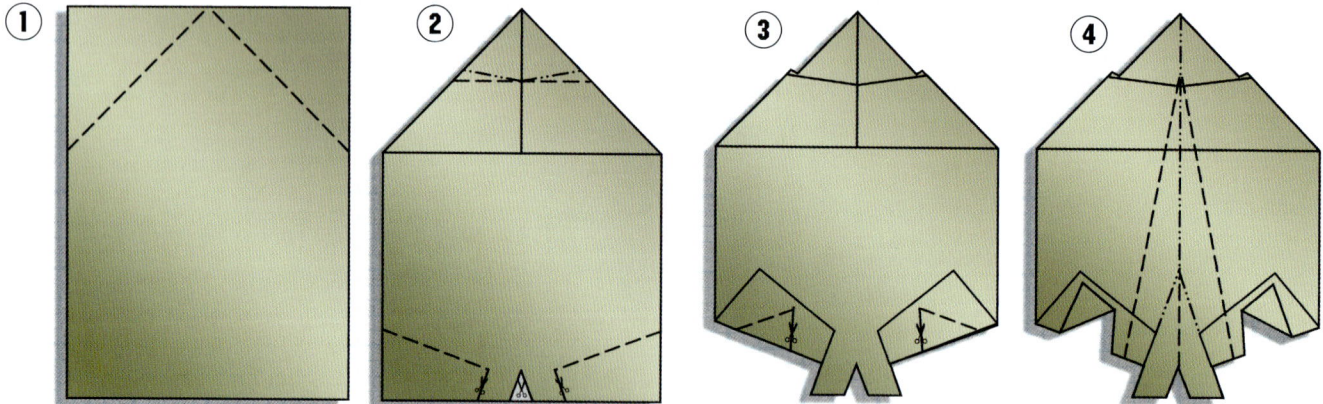

1. Fold in the two top corners using valley folds.

2. Fold down the top triangle using a valley fold. Next, make two mountain folds along the dashed lines by folding the pointed tip back on itself. Cut out the tail using the solid lines as your guide. Valley folds along the diagonal dotted lines form the rear of the wings.

3. Cut two slits along the solid lines. Then, using valley folds, bend along the diagonal lines, as shown.

4. Firmly fold the plane down its centre using a mountain fold, ensuring that the folds in the pointed tip stay securely tucked in place. Make sure you form a short valley fold between the two diagonal mountain folds at the rear. Fold down the wings along the long diagonals.

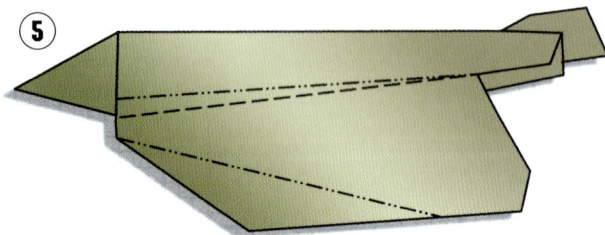

5. To form the main body and wings, use a series of valley and mountain folds as shown. Open out the tail fins.

To fly your plane, hold it about 6 cm from the front and throw it gently forwards.

FANTASTIC FLIERS FACT
The P-51 Mustang could outrun a Spitfire at low level, and fly three times as far.

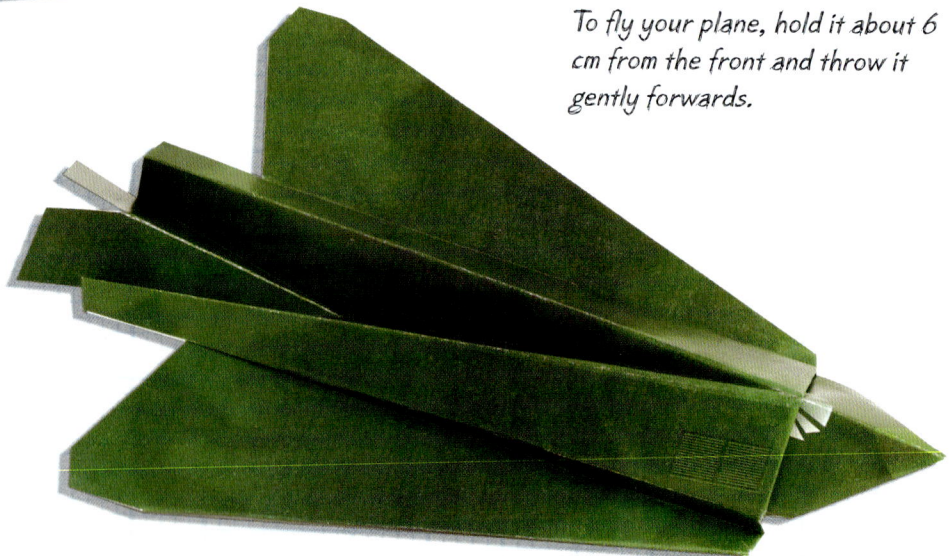

BAe SEA HARRIER

THIS JUMP JET GETS STRAIGHT OFF THE GROUND.
USE THE PRINTED PAGE NUMBERED 6 AT THE BACK OF THIS BOOK.

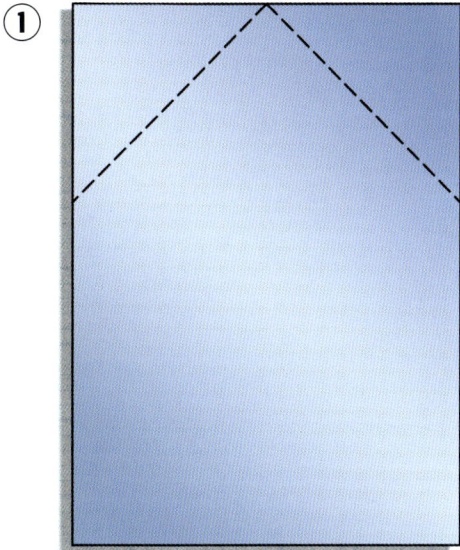

1. Fold in the two top corners along the dotted lines using valley folds.

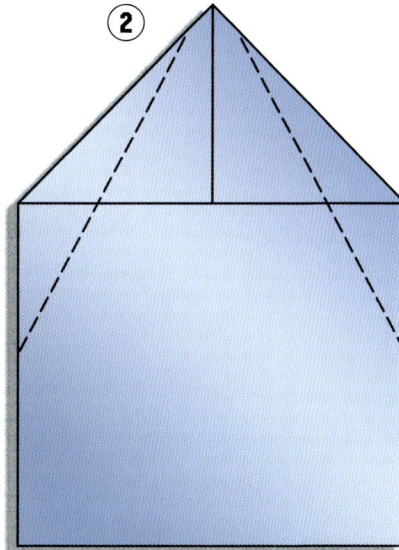

2. Fold along the two diagonal dotted lines, again using valley folds.

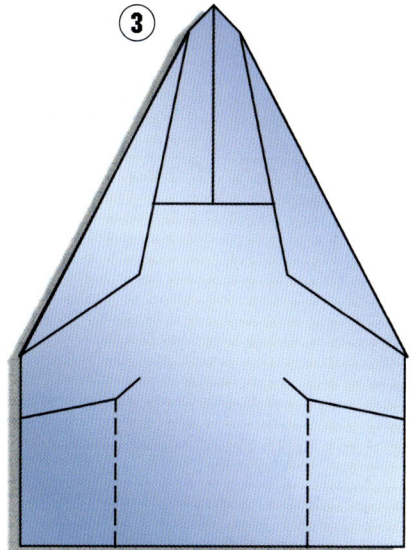

3. Cut two short angled lines along the solid lines on either side. Fold these flaps over using valley folds along the vertical lines, as shown. Make sure these flaps are kept tucked in for all of the following steps.

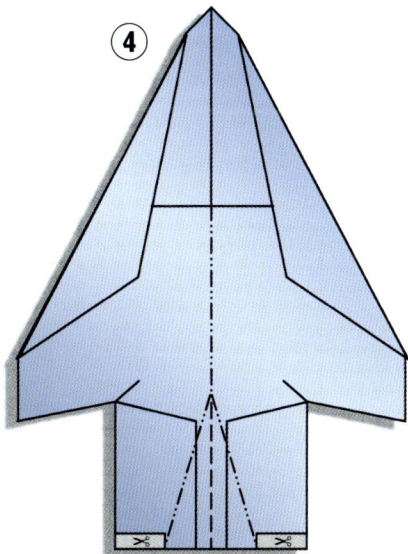

4. Cut out two small rectangles at the bottom by following the solid lines. Make mountain folds along the dashed lines and valley folds along the dotted lines to form the shape of the plane, as shown.

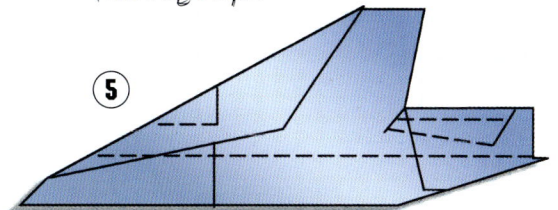

5. Make small slits by cutting along the solid lines on the wings and tail section, as shown. Using valley folds, create the main shape of the body and wings.

To fly your plane hold it about 5 cm from the front and throw it gently forward.

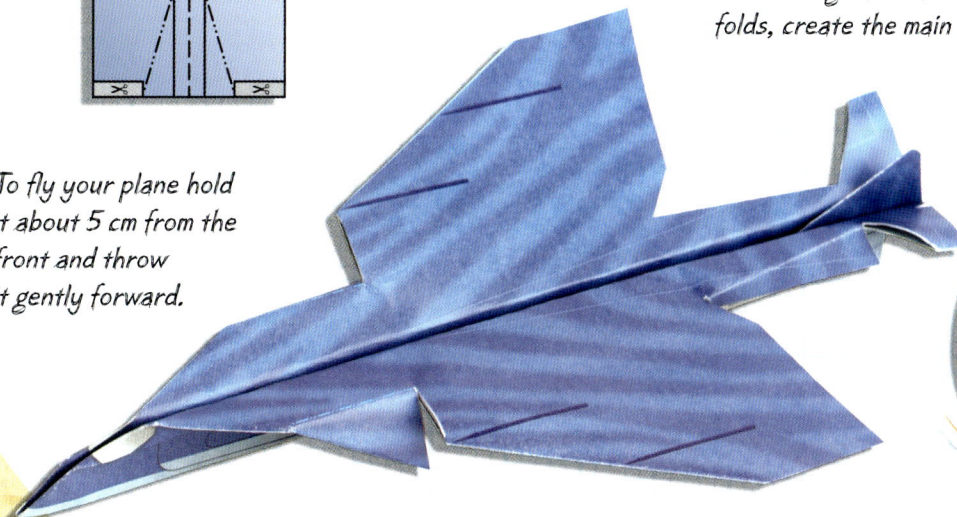

PANAVIA TORNADO IDS

THIS SPEEDY FIGHTER CAN BE CREATED IN MINUTES.
USE THE PRINTED PAGE NUMBERED 7 AT THE BACK OF THIS BOOK.

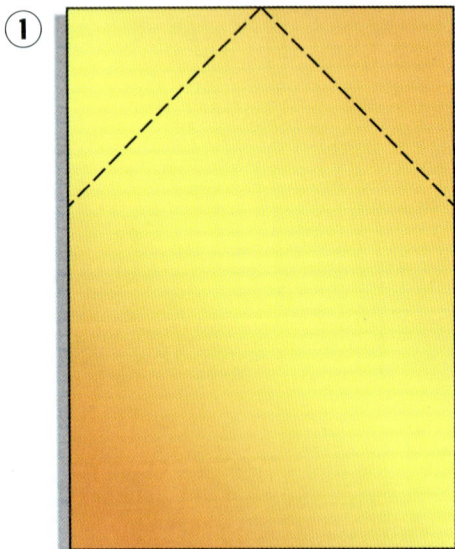

1. Fold in the two top corners along the dotted lines using valley folds.

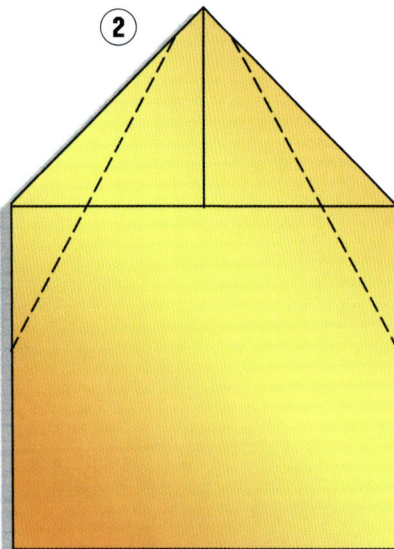

2. Fold along the two diagonal dotted lines, again using valley folds.

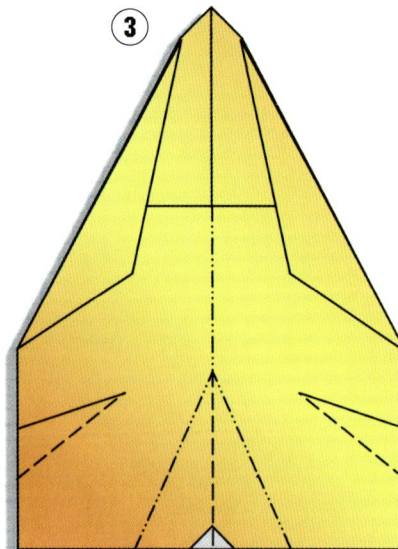

3. Cut along the four solid lines, as shown. Make mountain folds and valley folds to form the shape of the plane.

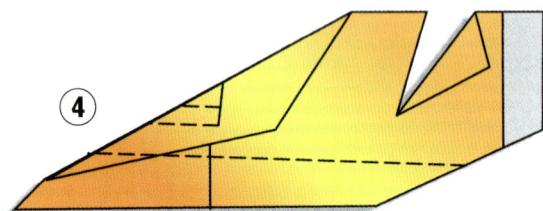

4. Cut off the end of the tail along the solid line. Then cut small slits on the wings along the solid lines, as shown. Using valley folds, form the tail, wings and body section.

To fly your plane hold it about 9 cm from the front and throw gently forwards.

FANTASTIC FLIERS FACT
The P-51 Mustang was an active fighter for over 30 years with air forces around the world.

DASSAULT MIRAGE IVP

MAKE THIS MARVELLOUS MIRAGE FIGHTER FOR YOUR MISSIONS.
USE THE PRINTED PAGE NUMBERED 8 AT THE BACK OF THIS BOOK.

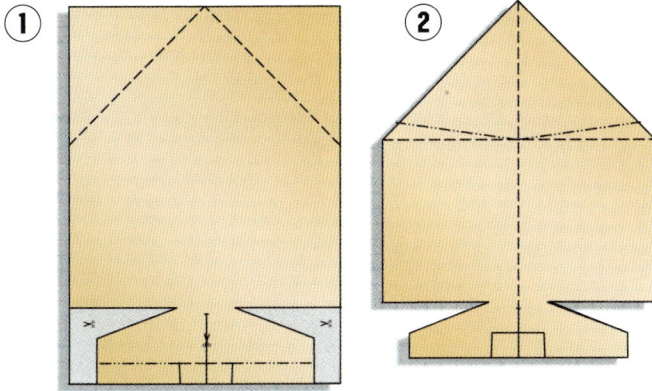

1. Fold in the two top corners along the dotted lines using valley folds. Cut three slits at the bottom along the solid lines. Cut away the surplus tail section. Fold the outer flaps under using mountain folds and the inner flaps out using valley folds.

2. Now fold the pointed tip towards you using a valley fold along the straight line. Next, make two mountain folds along the diagonal lines by folding the pointed tip back on itself. Firmly fold the plane down its centre, using a valley fold, ensuring that the folds in the pointed tip stay securely tucked in place.

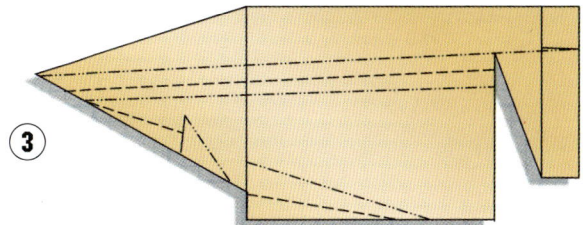

3. Cut a slit toward the front of the wings as indicated by another solid line. Then using a series of valley folds and mountain folds along the edges, form the basic shape of the plane.

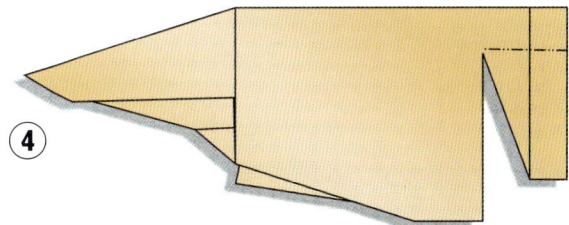

4. Fold up the wing tips using a valley fold and a mountain fold on each wing. Secure the tail by tucking the flap from one side around the other and interlock them.

To fly your plane, hold it about 8 cm from the front and throw it gently forwards.

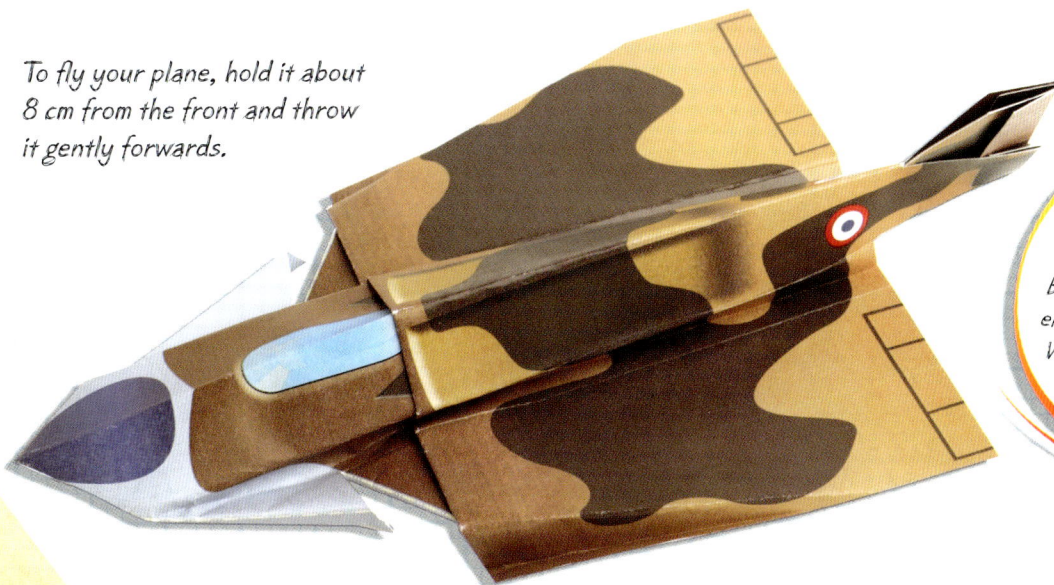

FANTASTIC FLIERS FACT
The Messerschmitt Bf-109 shot down more enemy aircraft in World War II than any other German aircraft.

LOCKHEED BOEING F-22

A GREAT JET FIGHTER MADE IN A FEW EASY STEPS.
USE THE PRINTED PAGE NUMBERED 9 AT THE BACK OF THIS BOOK.

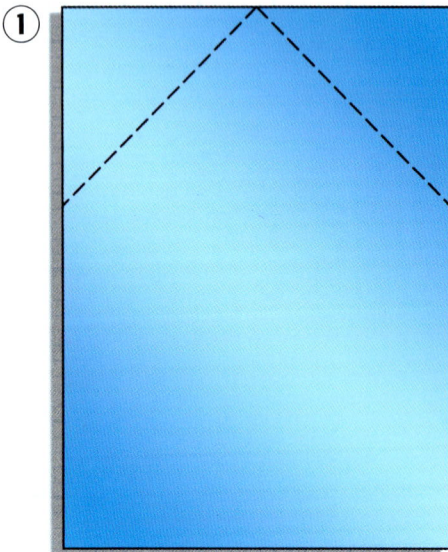

①

②

③

1. Fold in the two top corners along the dotted lines using valley folds.

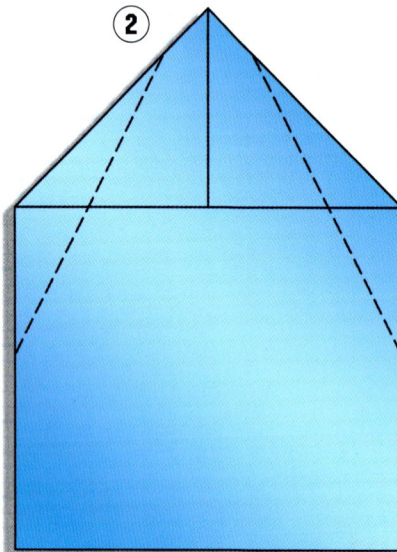

2. Fold along the two diagonal dotted lines, again using valley folds.

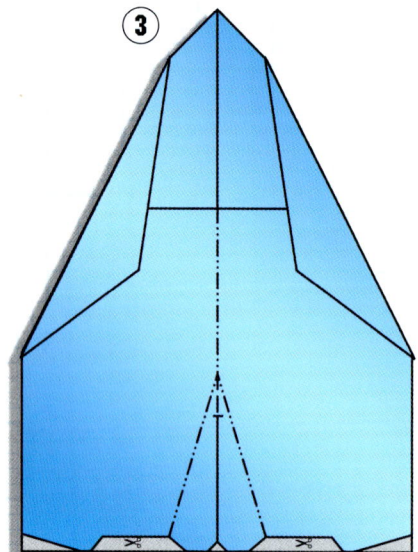

3. First, cut along the vertical solid line at the bottom. Cut away a small part of the tail along the solid lines, as shown. Make mountain folds and valley folds along the lines to form the shape of the plane.

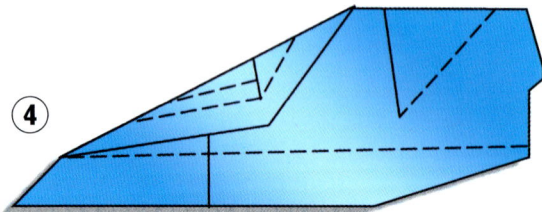

④

4. Make cuts on the wing along the solid lines. Valley folds along the dotted lines form the basic shape of the plane's body and wings.

FANTASTIC FLIERS FACT
The Fokker Wulf was built for air-to-air combat, and as a fighter bomber. It could carry cannon and machine guns – and up to three 500lb bombs.

To fly the plane hold it about 10 cm from the front and throw it gently forwards.

McDONNEL DOUGLAS F-15 EAGLE

THIS BIRD-LIKE PLANE WILL GLIDE WITH EASE.
USE THE PRINTED PAGE NUMBERED 10 AT THE BACK OF THIS BOOK.

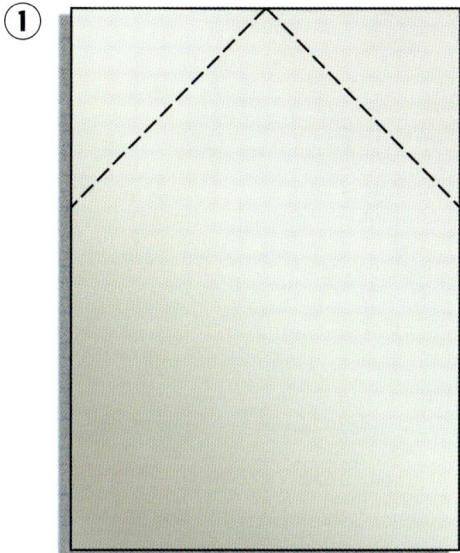

①

②

③

1. Fold in the two top corners along the dotted lines using valley folds.

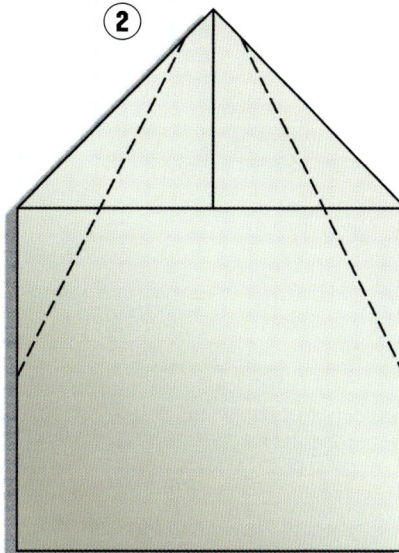

2. Fold along the two diagonal dotted lines, again using valley folds.

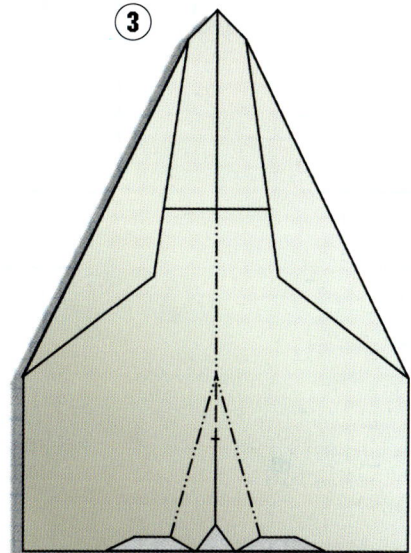

3. First cut along the vertical solid line at the bottom, as shown. Cut away the tail shape. Firmly fold the plane down its centre using a mountain fold. Make sure you form a short valley fold by the slit, between the rear mountain folds.

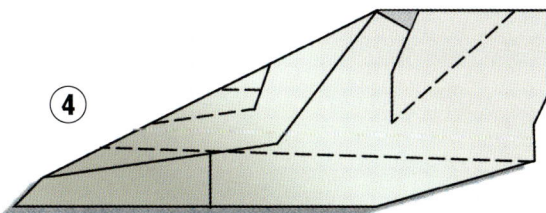

④

4. Make cuts on the wings along the solid lines, as shown. Using valley folds, fold along the dotted lines to create the shape of the wings.

To fly your plane hold it about 9 cm from the front and throw it gently forwards..

FANTASTIC FLIERS FACT
The Harrier Jump Jet uses swivelling nozzles on its engine to give it vertical lift.

MIG-23 FLOGGER

THIS RUSSIAN PLANE IS GREAT IN A DOGFIGHT.
USE THE PRINTED PAGE NUMBERED 11 AT THE BACK OF THIS BOOK.

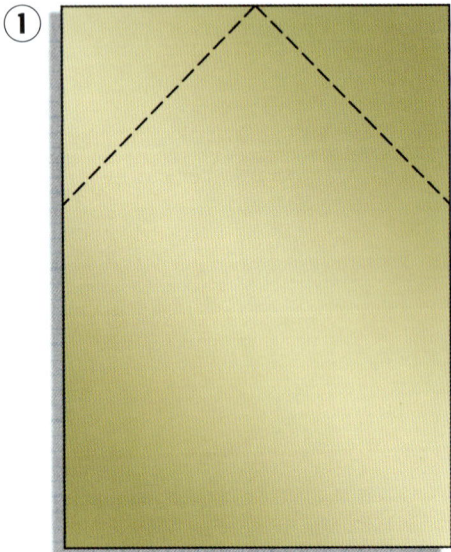

1. Fold in the two top corners along the dotted lines using valley folds.

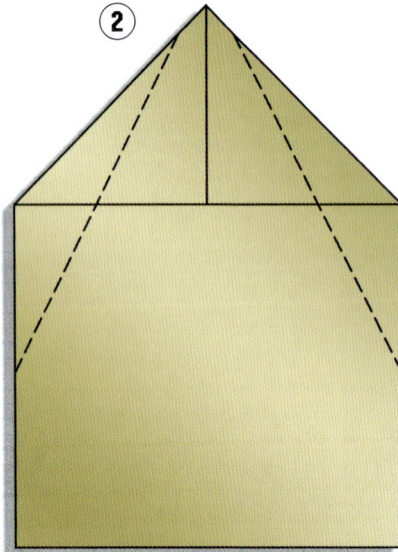

2. Fold along the two diagonal dotted lines, again using valley folds.

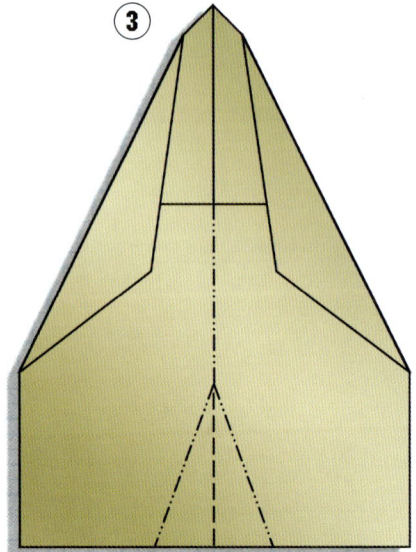

3. Fold the whole plane in two by making mountain folds along the centre line and the two small diagonals. Make a valley fold along the bottom section.

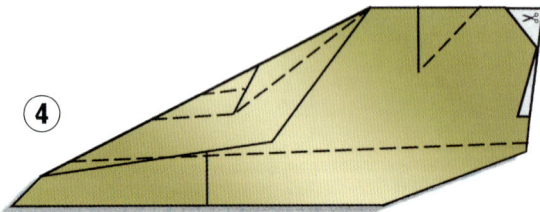

4. Cut away the tail by using the solid lines as a guide. Make cuts on the wings along the solid lines, as shown. Using valley folds, fold along the dotted lines to create the shape of the plane.

FANTASTIC FLIERS FACT
The Phantom F4 often flew from aircraft carriers. It had fold-back wings to take up less space.

To fly your plane hold it about 10 cm from the front and throw it gently forwards.

F-14 TOMCAT

THIS IMPRESSIVE F-14 TOMCAT WILL TEAR THROUGH THE SKY AT TOP SPEED.
USE THE PRINTED PAGE NUMBERED 12 AT THE BACK OF THIS BOOK.

1. Hold the page pattern-side down. Fold the top corners along the dotted lines using valley folds.

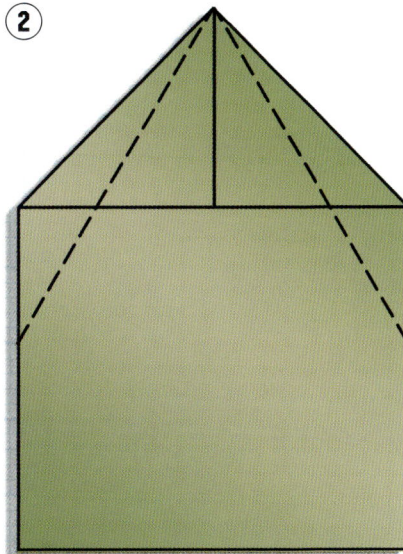

2. Make two more valley folds along the diagonal dotted lines.

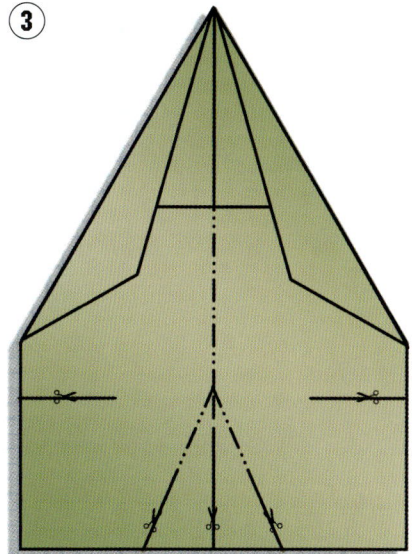

3. Using a pair of scissors, cut along the five solid lines as shown. Make a mountain fold along the central line running down the plane. Make valley folds on the lines either side of the central fold, making sure you form a short valley fold between the two diagonal mountain folds at the rear of the plane.

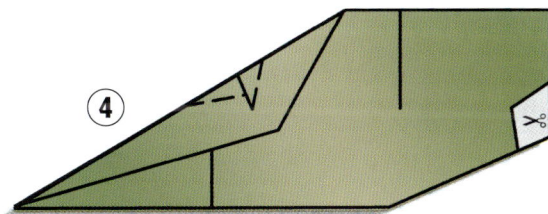

4. Next, cut around the tail area along the solid lines. Now make valley folds along the dotted lines.

5. Using diagonal valley folds, bend the flaps on the tail into place. Then, using more valley folds, form the wings on either side of the plane. Finally cut the tip off the tail and separate out.

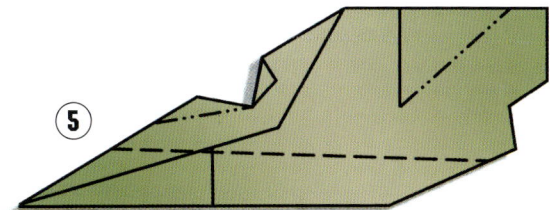

Hold the plane approximately 9 cm from the tip and throw gently.

FANTASTIC FLIERS FACT
The P51 Mustang flew fast, but was built fast, too. It only took 102 days to design and build the first P51!

SEPECAT JAGUAR

THE SENSATIONAL SEPECAT JAGUAR IS SUPER SPEEDY AND EASY TO MAKE.
USE THE PRINTED PAGE NUMBERED 13 AT THE BACK OF THIS BOOK.

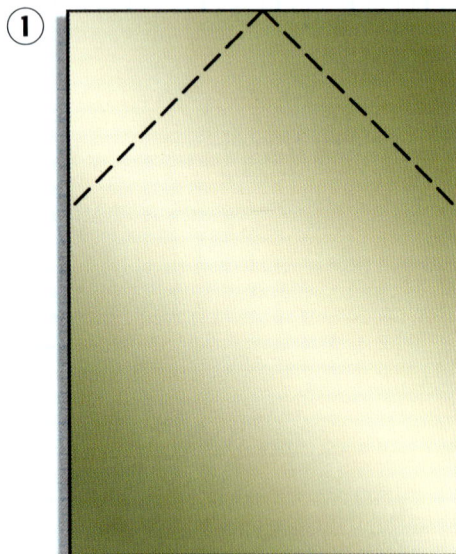

1. Hold the page pattern-side down. Using valley folds, fold the top corners along the dotted lines.

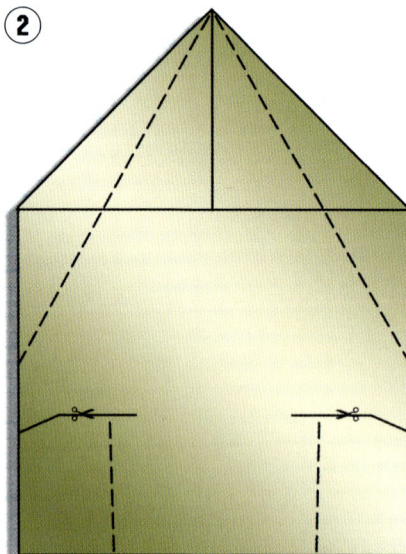

2. Make two more valley folds along the diagonal dotted lines. Using a pair of scissors, carefully cut along the solid lines. Now fold in the two flaps, along the dotted lines

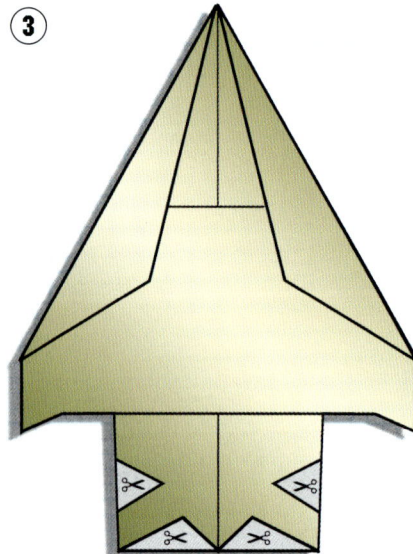

3. Using a pair of scissors, carefully cut away the four triangles to shape the tail fins.

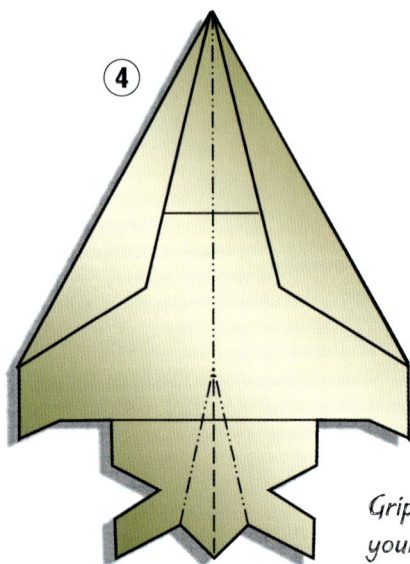

5. Next form the wings by making the remaining valley folds on both sides of the plane's body. Finish the tail with diagonal folds.

4. Fold in the tail along the vertical fold lines. Now make mountain folds along the three dashed lines running down the centre of the plane. Make sure you form a short valley fold between the two diagonal mountain folds at the rear, keeping the tail pieces tucked inside as you fold.

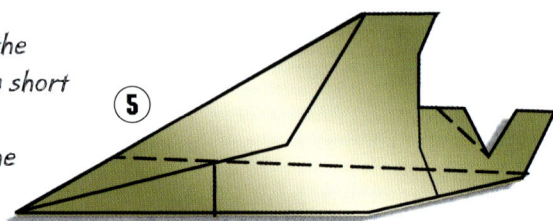

Grip the underside of your plane, approximately 9 cm from the tip and throw.

FANTASTIC FLIERS FACT
The Fokker DR.1 had three wings, and in WW1 could outclimb any other plane. It can hide in the sun, and surprise other aircraft from above.

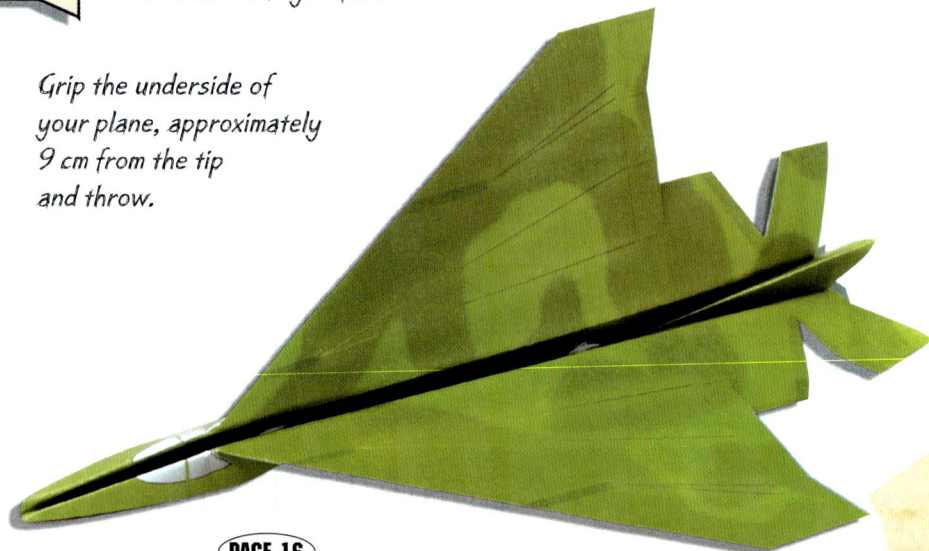

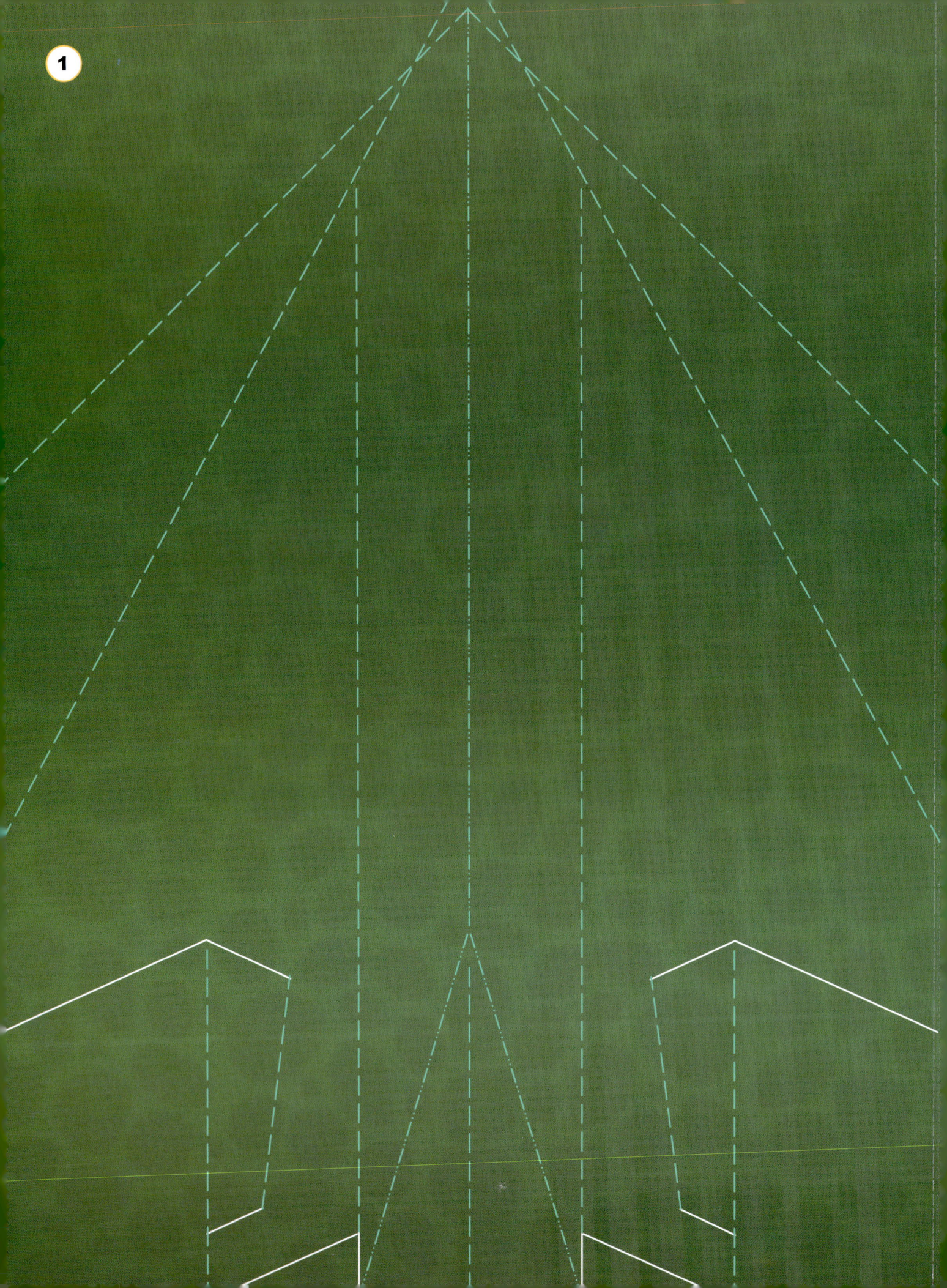

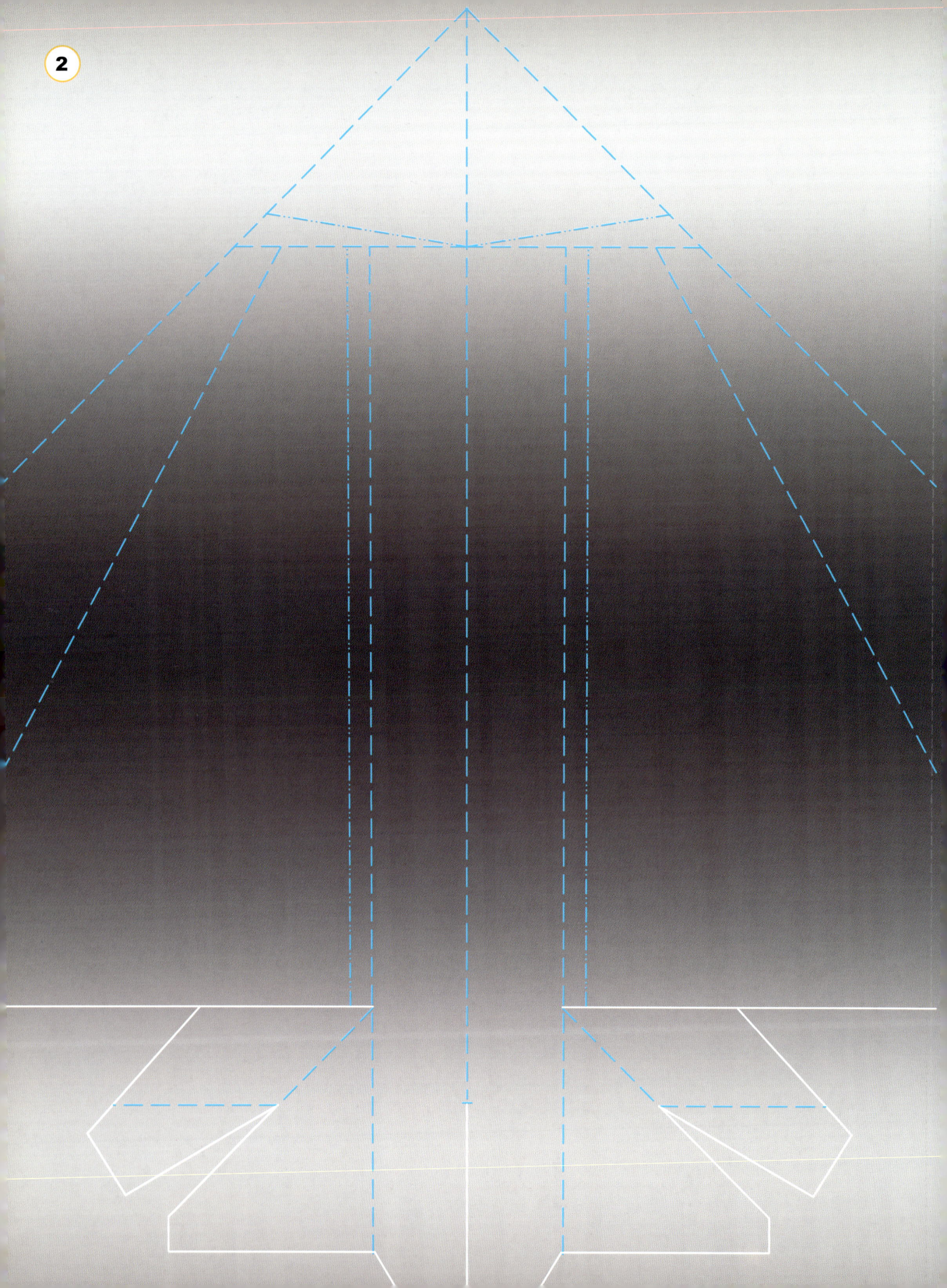

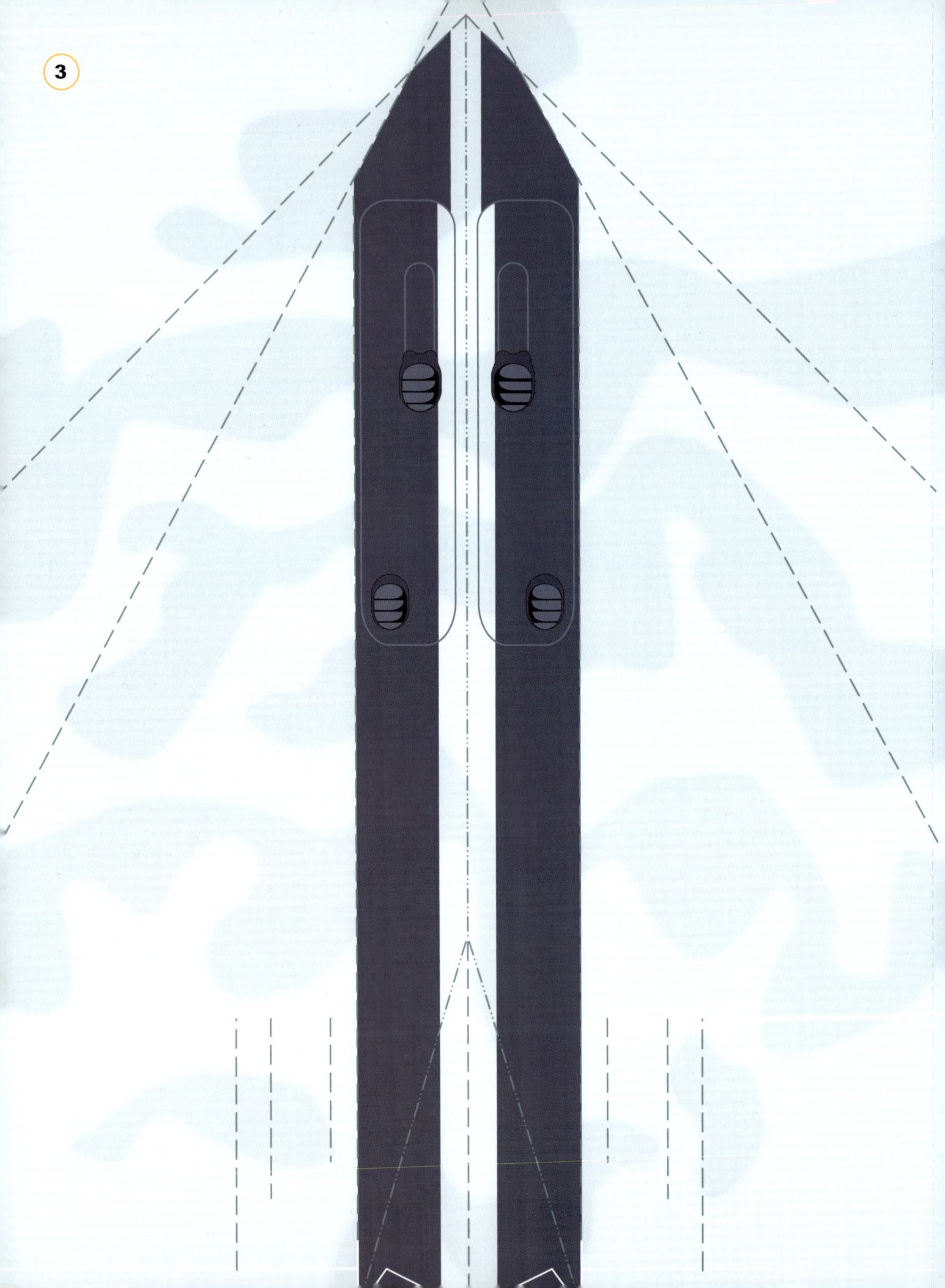

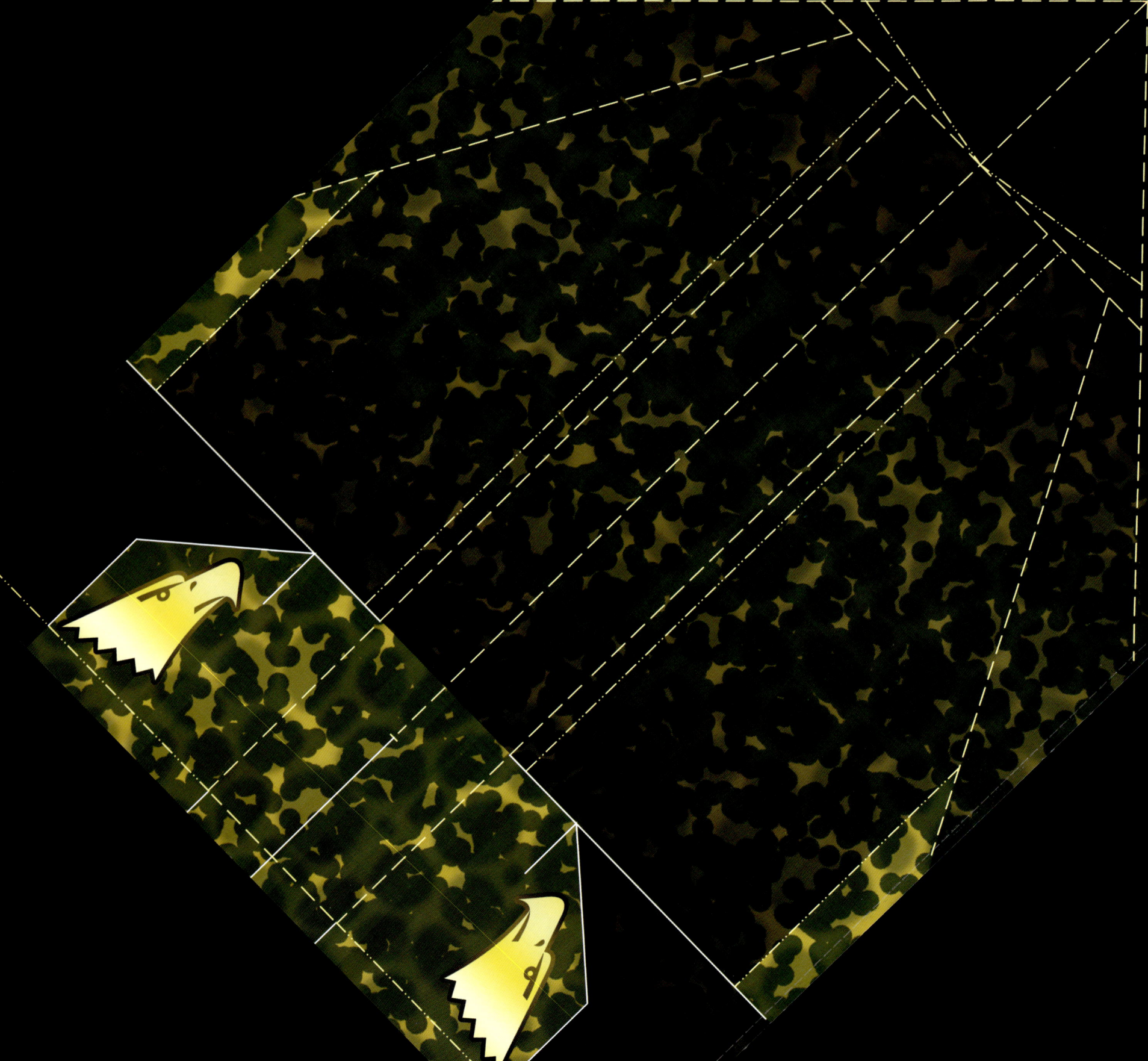

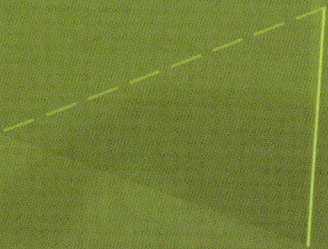

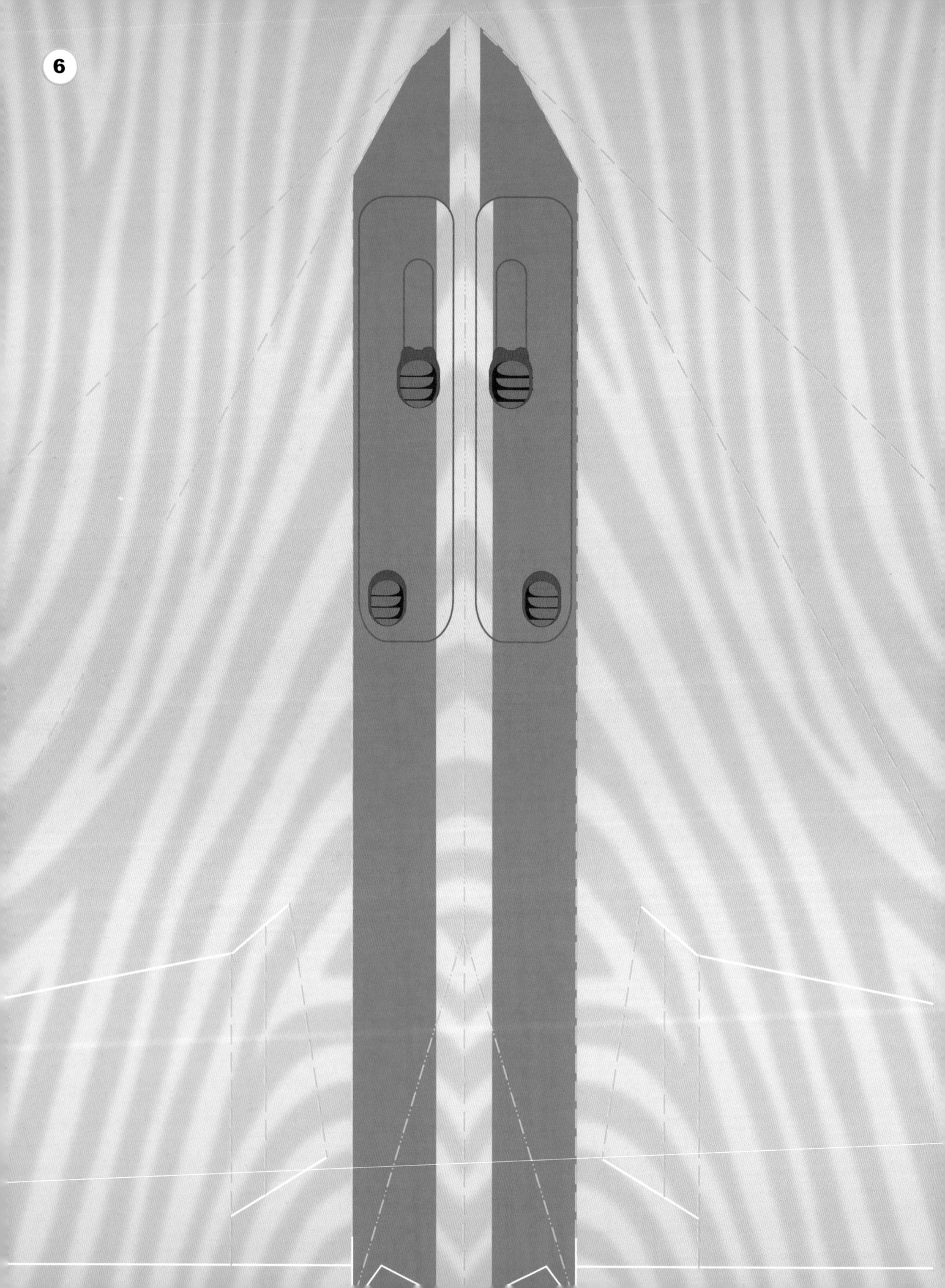

6

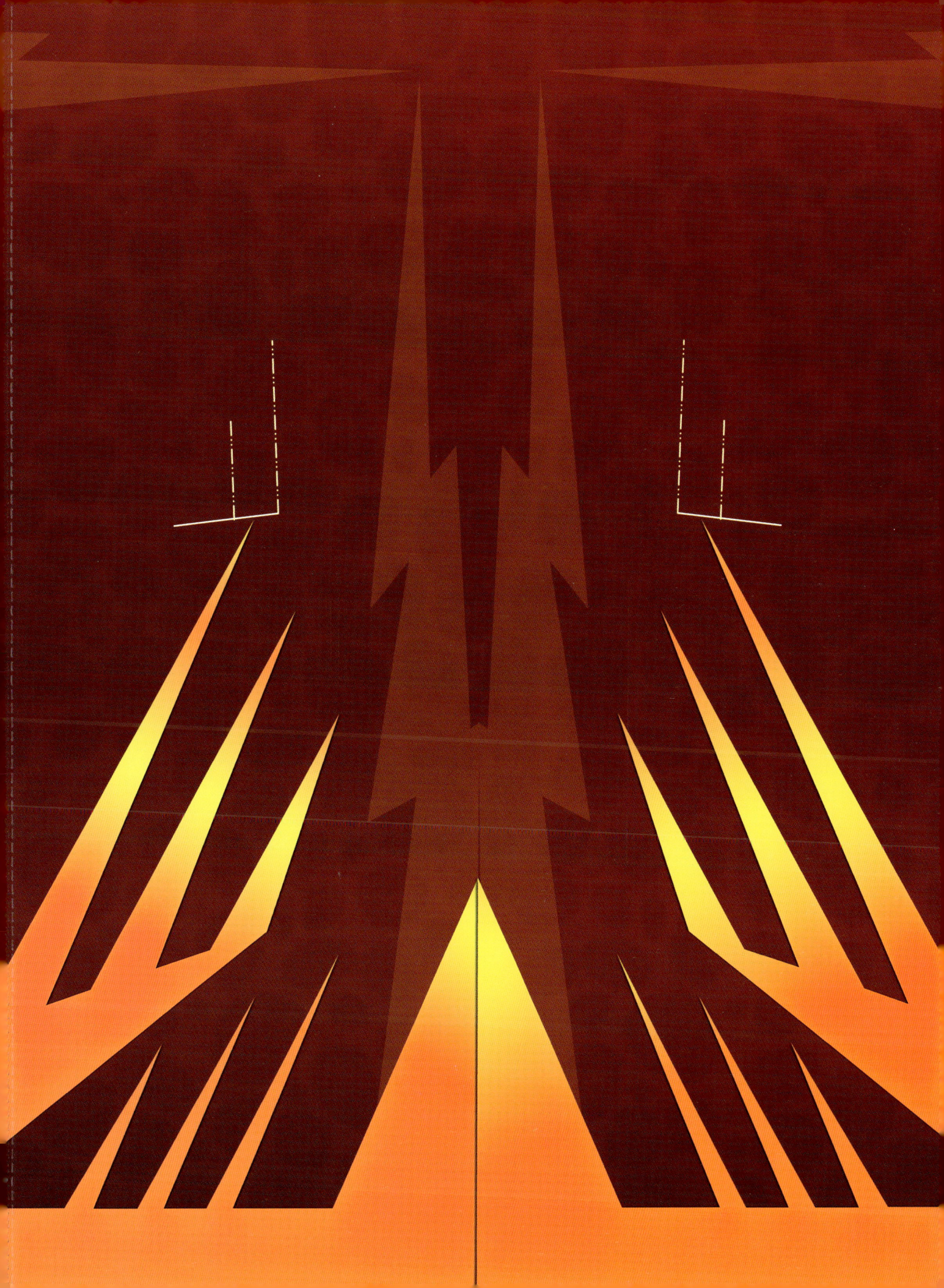

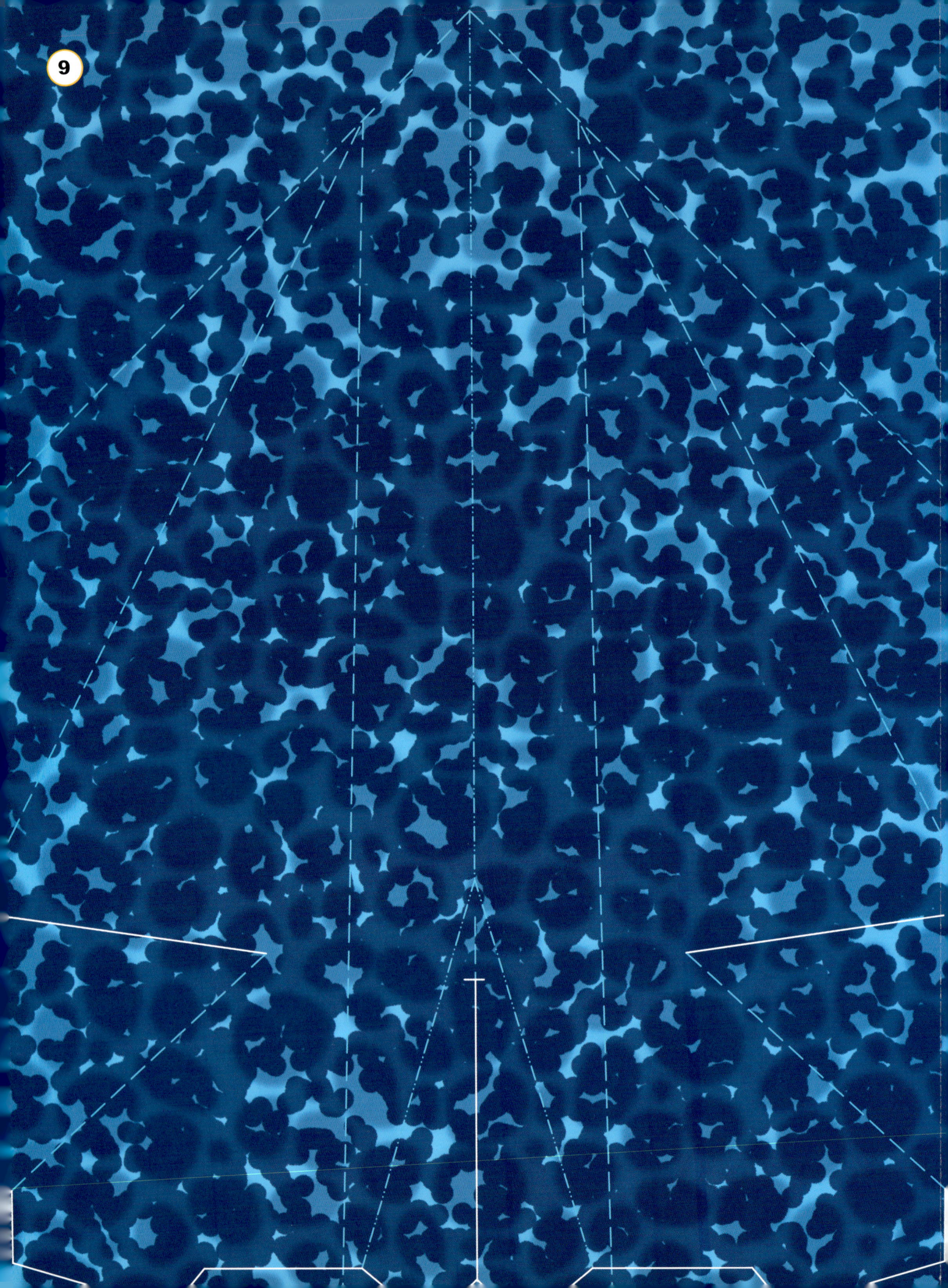

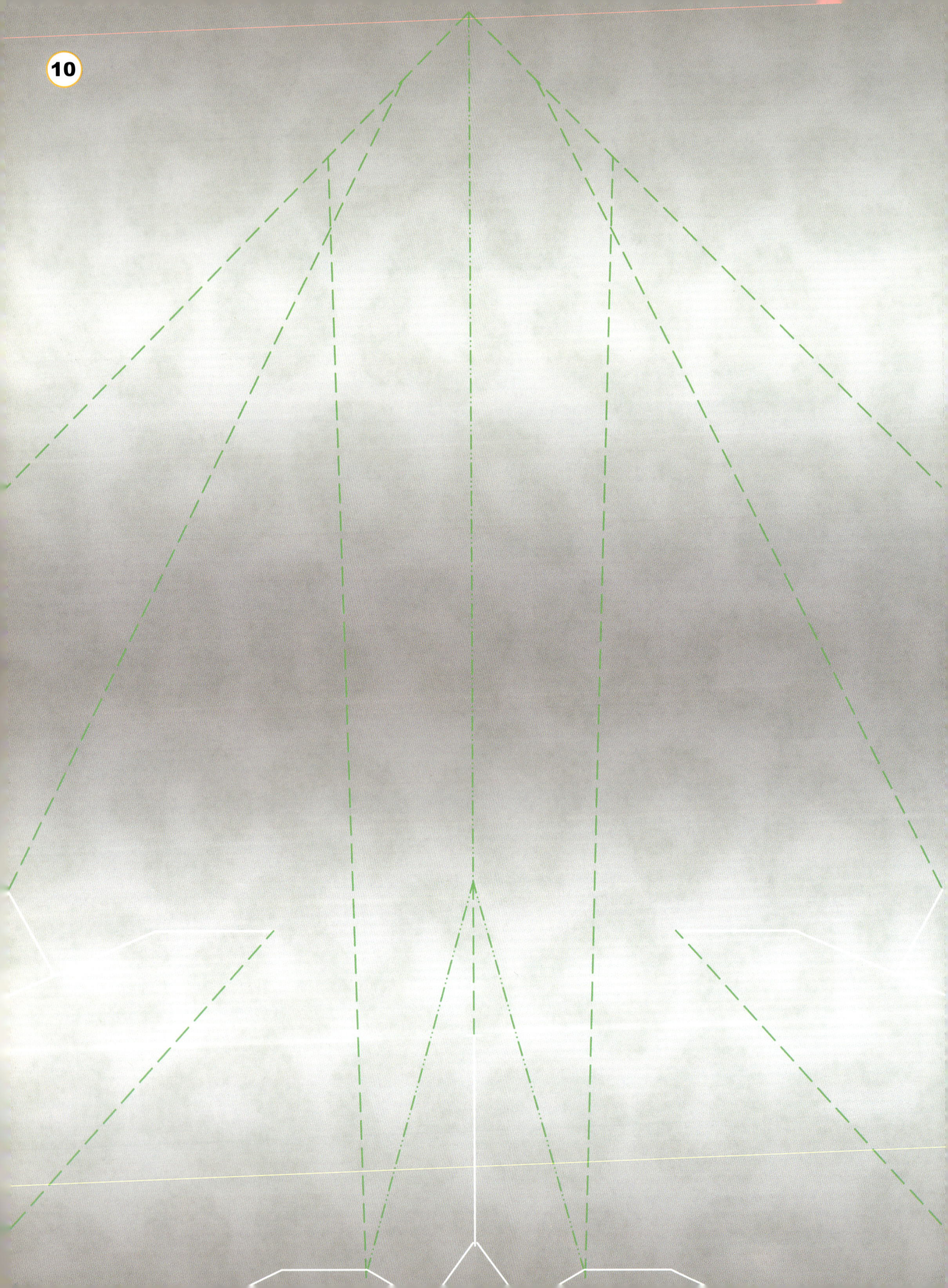

10

OOH OOH

12

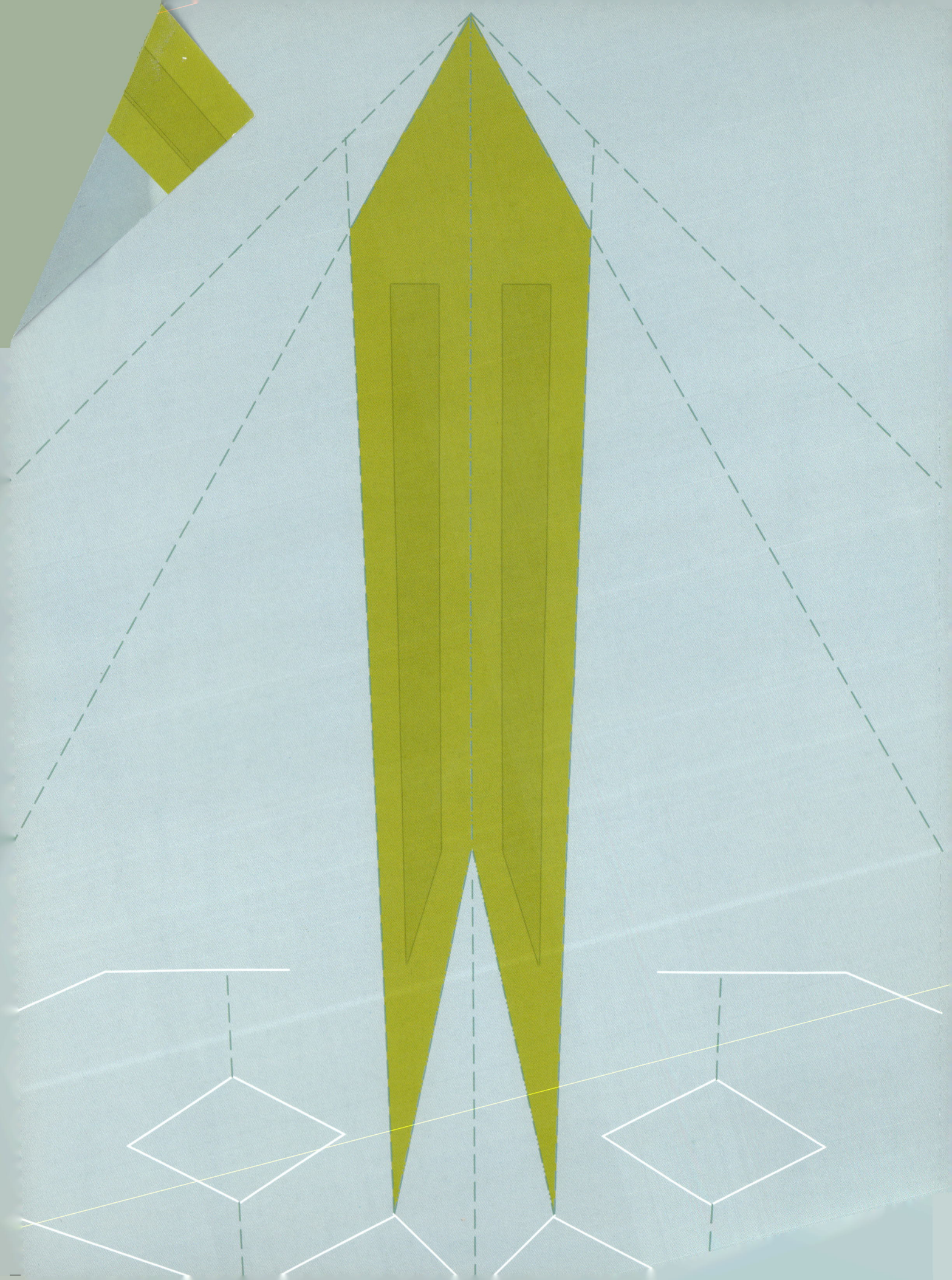

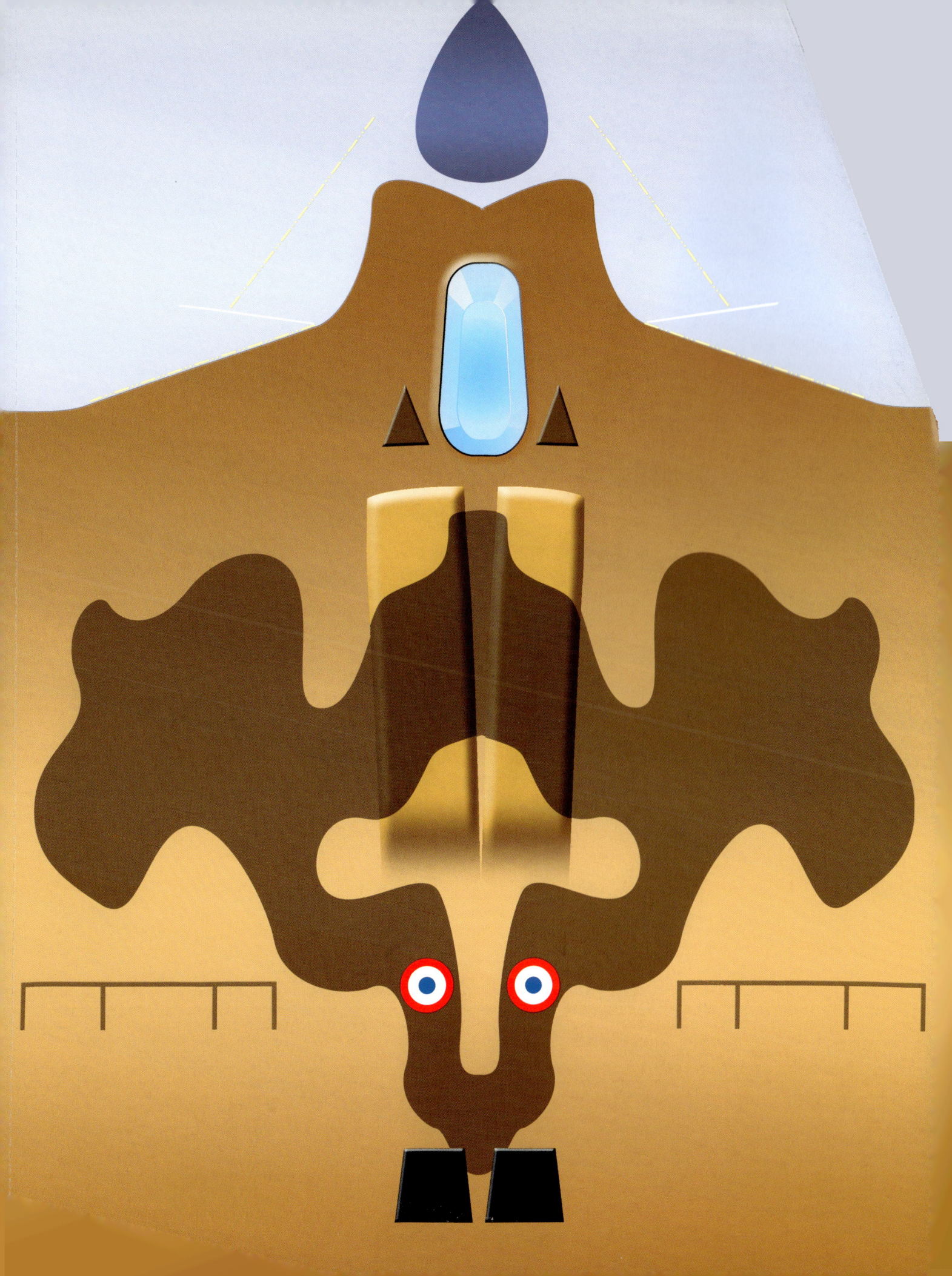

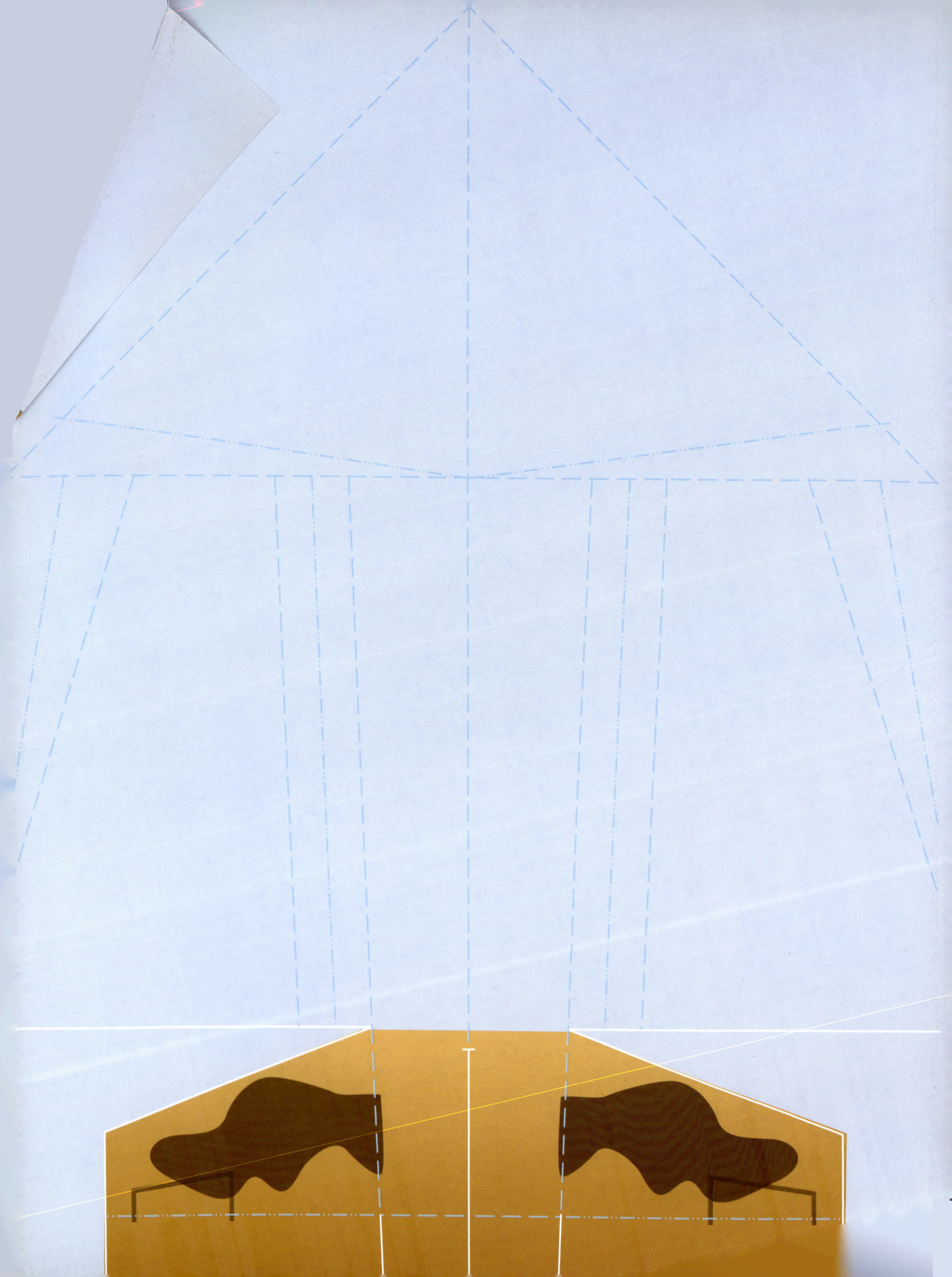

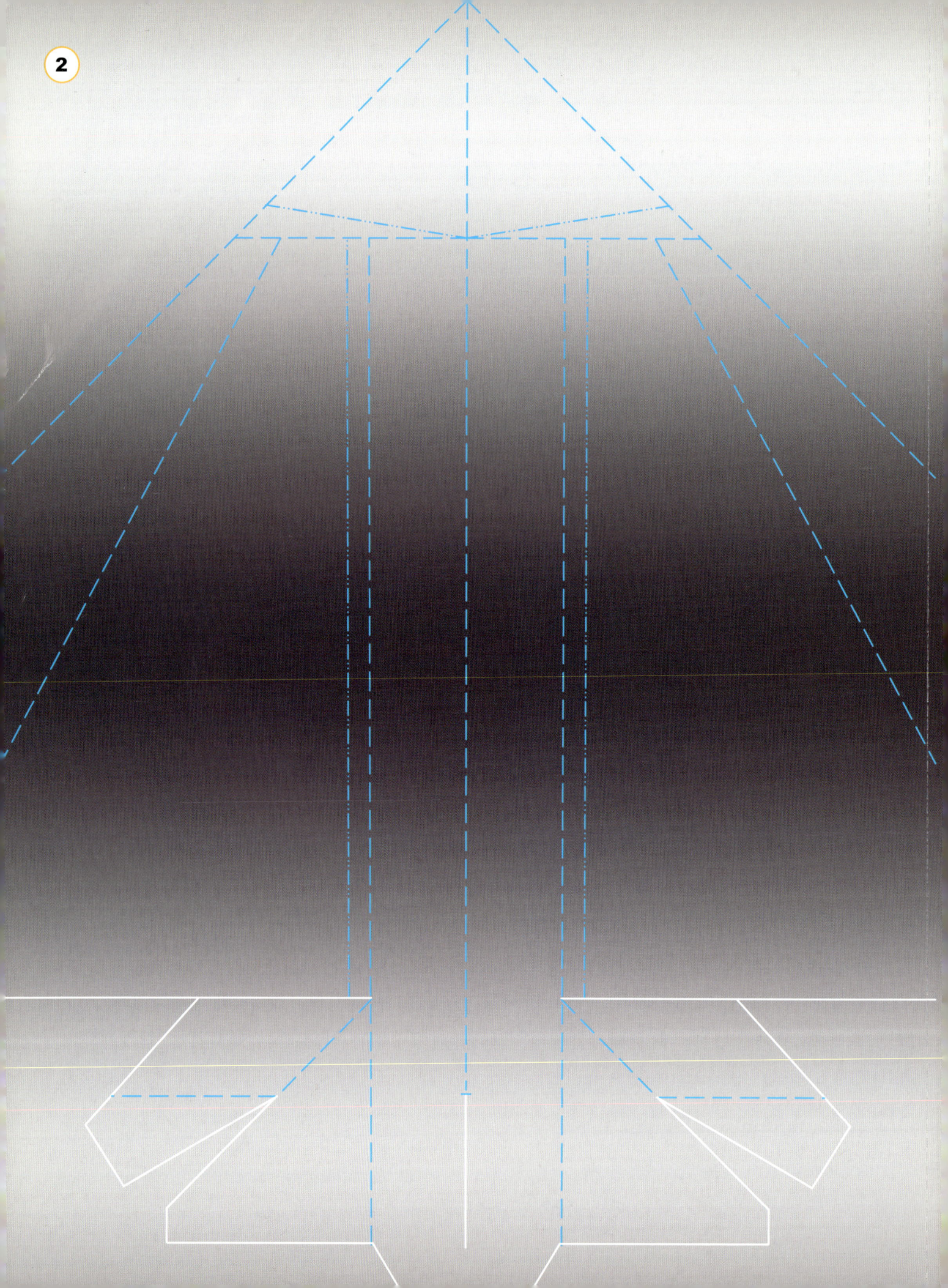